D1327764

BRAVERY IN WORLD WAR II

First published in 2013 by Wayland

Wayland
338 Euston Road
London NW1 3BH

Wayland Australia
Level 17/207 Kent Street
Sydney, NSW 2000

Editor: Annabel Stones
Designer: Elaine Wilkinson
Researchers: Laura Simpson and Edward Field
at The National Archives

The National Archives looks after the UK government's historical documents. It holds records dating back nearly 1,000 years from the time of William the Conqueror's Domesday Book to the present day. All sorts of documents are stored there, including letters, photographs, maps and posters. They include great Kings and Queens, famous rebels like Guy Fawkes and the strange and unusual – such as reports of UFOs and even a mummified rat!

Material reproduced courtesy of The National Archives, London, England.
www.nationalarchives.gov.uk

Catalogue references and picture acknowledgements (Images from The National Archives unless otherwise stated): Cover (photo left) & p.18: HS 9/612 Christine Granville, SOE agent, WWII; Cover (photo right)& p.9 (top right): INF 1/244 Battle of Britain pilots and air gunners, possibly from a Defiant Squadron; Cover (photo bottom right) & p.27 (top): ADM 203/94 (5) R M Commando at D-Day beach defences; Cover (centre, medal): © Crown copyright 2013; Title page & p.13: AIR 27/839 Operation Chastise Dambusters, Sqn Ldr Searby, Wg Cdr Gibson, Sqn Ldr Ward-Hunt; p.2 & p.11 (bottom): INF 3/0481 "Civilian Armament Instructor L Harrison" by RZ, 1943; p.4: MFQ 1/525 (101) King George VI meets pilots of Fighter Command; p.5 (top): Shutterstock; p.5 (middle): INF 3/0421 "Commander E.S Fogarty Fegen" Artist unknown, 1943; p.5 (bottom): FO 96/221 No302 Hitler speaks on anniversary of the Nazi revolution in the Reichstag; p.6, p.10, p.16, p22, p.24 & p.30: Shutterstock; p.7 (top): INF 3/0413 Captain H.M Ervine Andrews Artist unknown, 1943; p.7 (bottom): INF 3/1590 Effects of aerial bombardment on troop transport; p.8: AIR 4/21 David Crook's Spitfire; p.9 (top left): AIR 4/21 2 David Crook's Spitfire; p.11 (top): AIR 34/734 Beckton gasworks, Blitz; p.12: INF 2/42 (1002) Guy Gibson; p.13 (top): AIR 20/4367 Eder Dam after attack; p.14: Wikimedia Commons: Corporal (later Section Officer) Daphne Pearson GC of the Womens Auxiliary Air Force (WAAF); p.15 (top right): INF 3/403 Women for Industry Women of Britain. Come into the factories... Artist Zec; p.15 (bottom left): INF 3/0480 Aircraftsman Frost & Leading Aircraftsman Campion, Artist unknown, 1943; p.17 (top): INF 3/0130 "Convoy of British merchant ships" by Blake, Post-1941; p.17 (bottom): INF 2/1 pt 2 (516) Winston Churchill by Cecil Beaton; p.19 (top left): HS 7/135 SOE Resistance fighter plants explosives on a railway liine somewhere in France; p.19 (bottom right): HS 16/1 Christine Granville's code card 1944 (reverse); p.20: ADM 205/30 New U-Boat bunker with bomb-proof roof at St Nazaire; p.21 (top): DEFE 2/126 British forces captured at St Nazaire; p.21 (bottom): AIR 34/744 Tirpitz in Bogen fjord; p.23 (top): AIR 40/2292 Great Escape plan of surrounding area; p.23 (bottom right): AIR 40/229 Aerial photo of Stalag Luft III Sagan; p.25 (middle left): "Patrolling in jungle swamp" by Clive Uptton, 1944; p.25 (top right): AIR 23/4927 South-East Asia Jungle Kit checklist; p.26: ADM 203/94 (3) Beach obstacles D-Day; p.27 (bottom): INF 3/1571 Tank's crew surrendering to British infantry Artist Marc Stone; p.28 (left below): PREM 3/175 Crisis point reached in evacuation of BEF from Dunkirk; p.28 (right above): WO 106/1693 BEF in Dunkirk telegram; p.29 (top): E 31/2/2 f260r Great Domesday Book Shropshire; p.29 (bottom): Photoshoot 191census archive 3.

Background images and other graphic elements courtesy of Shutterstock.

A cataloguing record for this title is available at the British Library.

ISBN 978 0 7502 7973 4

Dewey Number 940.5'4'00922

Printed in China

Wayland is a division of Hachette Children's Books, an Hachette UK company
www.hachette.co.uk

CONTENTS

WHAT IS BRAVERY?

History is full of examples of bravery and courage. In a time of war, during a disaster, or in everyday life, we know stories of how ordinary people carry out the most remarkable feats of heroism. When people act heroically it is sometimes called going 'beyond the call of duty' because they do more than is expected of them.

▲ **King George VI meets pilots of Fighter Command.**

World War II was a horrific global conflict in which some human beings were ordered or expected to do the most terrible things. However, people often voluntarily risked their own lives to help or save somebody else. In this book you will see examples of ordinary people who have shown extraordinary courage.

As far back as the Roman Republic and Empire (508-29 BC), soldiers were decorated for acts of bravery and skill. In Britain, medals and ribbons have been awarded for gallantry since the 17th century. They are an expression of thanks to a person on behalf of the nation when someone does something selfless. They are also awarded to encourage and improve the morale of others. For example, if a member of a regiment wins the Victoria Cross there is a great sense of pride, not only in the individual, but also in the whole regiment, and even the whole country.

There are many different ways of recognising and rewarding acts of bravery. Some medals are awarded when a person acts in 'the face of the enemy', while others are given for bravery not in the front line of battle.

Remember that the people who received decorations during World War II were not the only brave people. There were many courageous acts that went unnoticed. Both servicemen and civilians who were in the front line helped each other without hesitating, even in life or death situations.

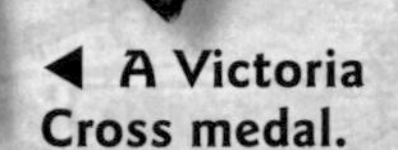

◀ **A Victoria Cross medal.**

'...for valour in giving his life and challenging hopeless odds to save the convoy of which he was in charge.'

'Captain Fegen could have, had he wished, turned to Southward with the remainder of the convoy in an endeavour to escape.'

◀ **Quotes taken from the request for a Victoria Cross for Captain Fegen.**

▲ **Merchant ships were easy targets for German U-boats and surface raiders.**

War with Germany

World War II (1939–45) broke out after Nazi Germany (led by Adolf Hitler, right) embarked on a policy of invading neighbouring countries. When Germany invaded Poland in September 1939, France and Britain declared war. The war became global when Germany invaded the Soviet Union (Russia) in June 1941. Soon after, Japan (Germany's ally) attacked the American naval base at Pearl Harbour, and then parts of the British Empire such as Burma, Malaya and Hong Kong.

DUNKIRK EVACUATION

In May 1940, German forces unleashed a devastating attack against the British and French armies in Belgium and northern France, forcing them to retreat to the coast. Most troops made for the port of Dunkirk where the Royal Navy was organising an evacuation.

Name: Captain Harold Ervine-Andrews

Date: 31 May–1 June 1940

Event: Dunkirk Evacuation

Age: 28

Location: France

Medal: Victoria Cross

Date Awarded: 30 July 1940

Some troops formed a rearguard to slow down the attackers and buy time for those escaping. On 31 May, Captain Harold Ervine-Andrews led a company whose job was to protect a 900-metre-long defensive line in front of Dunkirk. Using a canal as a barrier, they dug in and – despite heavy artillery, mortar and machine-gun fire – held firm for ten hours.

However, German troops crossed the canal and threatened to surround their position. Ervine-Andrews, with cover from his men, climbed onto the roof of a thatched barn. Using his rifle and a light machine gun, he held the attackers back. Under the heavy fire, the barn caught fire.

Having run out of ammunition, Ervine-Andrews rejoined his men and sent the wounded to Dunkirk in a troop carrier. With eight of his company he kept up the resistance, but when almost surrounded again had to retreat. His company began wading through chin-high water and mud towards Dunkirk. Finding a safe place, he took up a defensive position and continued firing at the enemy.

Ervine-Andrews and his company's brave resistance slowed down the advancing Germans and allowed nearly 250,000 British and French troops to evacuate from Dunkirk. The group finally made it to the beaches near Dunkirk and escaped on 4 June – the last day of the evacuation.

▲ **Captain Ervine-Andrews 'holding the line' around Dunkirk.**

His Victoria Cross recommendation read: 'Ervine-Andrews displayed courage, tenacity and devotion to duty...and his magnificent example (inspired) his own troops with the fighting spirit which he himself displayed.'

A SECOND THOUGHT

How would you feel about still fighting while your comrades were escaping back to Britain?

Blitzkrieg

The German Army attacked the Allies using a new tactic – 'blitzkrieg'– which means 'lightning war'. This involved using three waves of attack. First, dive bombers terrorised and weakened the targets with concentrated aerial bombardment. Secondly, tanks rushed in to attack the confused defenders and smashed trough to their objectives. Thirdly, troops were quickly transported to the battle zone by vehicles and mopped up any remaining resistance.

▲ **This drawing shows the effects of aerial bombardment.**

THE BATTLE OF BRITAIN

In the summer of 1940 Hitler planned an invasion of Britain - Operation Sealion. To succeed he would have to destroy the Royal Air Force (RAF), otherwise his troop barges could not safely cross the English Channel. That summer saw RAF Fighter Command fighting for survival...

Name: David Moor Crook
Date: July–October 1940
Event: The Battle of Britain
Age: 25
Location: Southern England
Medal: Distinguished Flying Cross
Date Awarded: 1 November 1940

Pilot David Moor Crook joined 609 Squadron in 1938 and when war broke out he was made full Pilot Officer. On 10 July 1940, the Luftwaffe started their attacks on fighter stations. 609 Squadron's Spitfires were sent to RAF Warmwell in Dorset – right in the front line.

Every morning his section of pilots would gather in a hut near the aircraft and wait for the phone call that told them to 'Scramble!' – dash for their planes and get airborne quickly. While gaining altitude they would search the skies for enemy planes. The Spitfire pilots would try to attack the bombers, whose fighter escorts would try to stop them. Crook found himself trying to react in an instant to avoid collisions, lining up his gun sights and pressing the 'fire' button at the right time. He had to make sure he was at the right altitude – too low and he was defenceless against attack. These air battles between fighter planes were known as dogfights.

▼ David Crook's Spitfire takes off for London during the Battle of Britain.

▲ David Crook in his Spitfire.

Another strain, apart from dogfights, was the death of fellow pilots. Crook lost many close friends in the battle. Planes could be replaced but, as he wrote, there were 'So many attacks to meet and so few pilots to do it'. As the weeks passed he became wiser, learning from his mistakes. In one instance, he missed a Bf 110 fighter because he closed in too fast, overshooting the target. However, he was successful at other times, shooting down six enemy fighters – one Ju 87 ('Stuka'), three Bf 110s and two Bf 109s.

In October, Crook was awarded the Distinguished Flying Cross, for 'leading his section with coolness and judgement'. This award made Crook feel 'better than I've ever felt!'

▲ 609 Squadron was based at Northolt in west London between May and June 1940.

Victory

Had the RAF pilots not withstood the onslaught of the Luftwaffe, Germany might have invaded Britain in 1940. As Winston Churchill said, 'Never in the field of human conflict was so much owed, by so many, to so few'. The Battle of Britain was Hitler's first defeat since the invasion of Poland and it was a huge morale booster for the British people. Britain was the only country still at war with Germany and felt very isolated. If it was to attract support from the USA, it had to prove it would not be defeated.

A SECOND THOUGHT

What do you think the mood would be like in the hut as the pilots waited for the phone to ring?

BLITZ!

After failing to destroy the RAF, Hitler's Luftwaffe changed tactics. They decided to bomb key areas of population and industry. However, many bombs did not explode. To make safe one of these unexploded bombs - UXBs as they were called - required skill and courage of the highest order.

Name:
Leonard Harrison

Date:
14 February–7 June 1940

Event: The Blitz

Age: 35

Location: Lincolnshire

Medal: George Cross

Date Awarded:
3 January 1941

Leonard Harrison was an Armaments Instructor at an RAF training school in Mamby, Lincolnshire. On 12 February 1940, he and his colleague Flight Lieutenant John Dowland were called to the nearby port of Immingham.

A ship carrying much-needed grain had limped into dock with an unexploded bomb stuck in the deck. If the bomb exploded, the ship would sink, blocking the port and the food supplies would be lost. Some German bombs had a delayed action and exploded many hours after they had been dropped. The explosion would be detonated by a fuse, which had to be made safe. Unfortunately, many bombs were designed with anti-handling devices that were designed to detonate when bomb disposal crews worked on them.

Harrison first listened to the bomb for any ticking and then realised it had a new type of fuse he had never seen before. One wrong move could have blown the ship and everybody on it sky-high. Showing great coolness, Harrison gently loosened the fuse and, with amazing skill, made the device safe. Then, with help, he carried the bomb off the ship. He repeated this bravery again when a new type of depth charge was found on some trawlers (fishing boats) anchored near Grimsby in March and again in June 1940.

Strategic Bombing

The Luftwaffe's bombing of Britain was not random. Cities with factories making guns, tanks, aeroplanes and vehicles were hit hard, as were the nearby houses of the workers. London, Coventry, Birmingham, Belfast and Manchester were heavily bombed. Railways, goods yards, shipyards and docks were also targeted, so Glasgow, Liverpool, Cardiff, Hull and Plymouth endured devastating air raids. Bombing killed around 60,000 civilians during World War II.

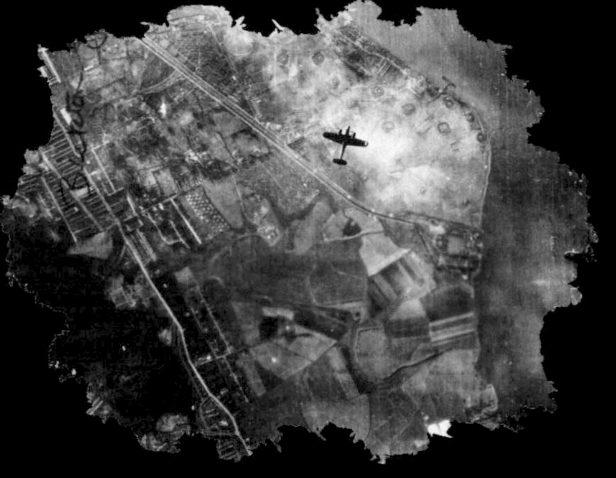

▲ A bomber from the Luftwaffe raids London.

Harrison became an expert on fuse and exploder systems. His knowledge also helped devise methods to stop fuse mechanisms from working. One way was to take all the air out of the fuse and replace it with a liquid that jammed the mechanism, and another was to use strong magnets which stopped the timers.

A SECOND THOUGHT

What qualities do you think were needed for work in bomb disposal?

▼ Leonard Harrison gently assesses the UXB on board the grain ship.

DAM BUSTERS

With no Allied forces fighting in northwest Europe, bombing raids on Germany became more important. Strategic targets were chosen to try and damage Germany's war effort...

Name: Flight Lieutenant Leslie Knight

Date: 16–17 May 1943

Event: Dam Busters Raid

Age: 22

Location: Ruhr Valley, Germany

Medal: Distinguished Service Order

Date Awarded: 25 May 1943

One of the most daring bombing raids of the war was Operation Chastise, the bombing of dams near the industrial heartland of Germany – the Ruhr Valley. If the dams could be broken, flooding would damage factories and reduce Germany's industrial output.

▲ Wing Commander Guy Gibson VC, Commanding Officer of 617 Squadron.

617 Squadron was set up in great secrecy to carry out the raid. One of the pilots was Australian Flight Lieutenant Leslie Knight.

By the end of March 1943 training for the raid had begun. Knight's Lancaster (N-Nan) plane would drop a new bomb designed by the engineer Barnes Wallis. The bomb would bounce on the lake, hit the dam and spin to the bottom and explode! All this meant very hard and dangerous training, but Knight was an excellent pilot. He had to fly low, at the right speed and be aware of the surrounding hills. Knight was in the first formation, flying with the raid leader Wing Commander Guy Gibson.

The raid took place on the night of 16–17 May and first formation took off at 9.39 pm. Their route avoided all known German anti-aircraft gun sites. Incredibly, the planes flew at 30 metres all the way!

The Mohne Dam was attacked first and then the formation headed towards the second target, the Eder Dam. After 12 minutes they lined up to attack. The dam was hit but didn't break, so it was down to Knight. With his crew on full alert, he flew in low, holding his line, despite the anti-aircraft fire exploding all around him. The bomb was released and as the plane climbed above the surrounding hills the crew looked back and saw the dam destroyed!

▲ **An impressive photograph of the Eder Dam after the attack.**

A SECOND THOUGHT

Imagine that you are a person at home in Britain during the war. How do you think you would have felt reading about the Dam Busters Raid?

Was it a Success?

Although two of the dams were broken and massive flooding took place, the damage to German industry was not as great as expected. The dams were repaired fairly quickly. However, there were serious losses of electrical power in Germany and coal production fell. Also, agricultural land was destroyed causing a serious drop in food output. The raid was a major propaganda victory because of its technical brilliance, however 617 Squadron lost 53 airmen.

▲ **Pilots who assisted with Operation Chastise.**

WOMEN'S WAR WORK

When war broke out, women were encouraged to help the war effort. Many went into factories to produce weapons. Others joined the armed forces, such as the Women's Auxiliary Air Force (WAAF), the Women's Royal Navy and the Auxiliary Territorial Services.

Name: Daphne Pearson

Date: 31 May 1940

Event: Plane crash

Age: 29

Location: RAF Detling, Kent

Medal:
Empire Gallantry Medal, converted to the George Cross

Date Awarded: 19 July 1940

▲ Daphne Pearson in her WAAF uniform.

Daphne Pearson was determined to 'do her bit' for the war effort and joined the WAAF as an assistant nurse. She was posted to RAF Detley in Kent, which was home to 500 Squadron.

At about 1 am on the morning of 31 May, Daphne was woken up by the sound of a plane in trouble. One of the engines had failed and it was trying to reach the airstrip. She watched in horror as the plane hit some trees and crashed. She ran towards the plane to help.

At the scene, some men were trying to drag the pilot clear. Daphne told them she would help the pilot and they should clear the way for the ambulance. She was pulling the injured pilot from the wreck, when he whispered that there were bombs on board. Suddenly, the fuel tank blew up and Daphne used her body to protect him from the blast. Then a 120 pound-bomb exploded, but she still protected him. A third explosion followed that knocked everyone over.

When the ambulance took the pilot, Daphne tried to rescue another crew member, but sadly he was already dead. She carried on helping the doctor through the night and still reported for duty at 8 am that morning.

Daphne was awarded the Empire Gallantry Medal and was praised in the House of Commons by Prime Minister Winston Churchill. In 1941 her medal was converted to the new George Cross and Daphne was the first woman recipient.

▲ This propaganda poster encouraged women to help with the war effort.

Working Women

When war broke out, men were conscripted into the armed forces. This meant there was a huge labour shortage so it was hoped women could fill the gaps. In 1941, women were also conscripted into essential war work and the armed forces, where they did everything from catering to working in anti-aircraft units. One obstacle was what women would do with children too young for school. By 1943, there were 1,450 local authority nurseries with places for 65,000 children.

▲ The scene that greeted Daphne when she reached the crash site.

SECOND THOUGHT

to imagine what Daphne was thinking as she ran towards the crashed plane.

ARCTIC CONVOYS

On 22 June 1941, the German Army invaded Russia (then called the Soviet Union). This gave Britain a powerful ally in the war against Hitler's Germany. It was agreed that Britain would send convoys of essential war equipment to help Russia continue the fight effectively.

Name:
Loftus Peyton-Jones

Date: 31 December 1942

Event: Arctic Convoy

Age: 24

Location: The Barents Sea

Medal: Distinguished Service Order

Date Awarded:
23 February 1943

The journey to Russia involved a terrible journey across the freezing Arctic Ocean to reach the northern ports of Murmansk and Archangel in northwest Russia. These convoys needed constant protection from attack by German warships, submarines (U-boats) and aeroplanes. These were based in Norway, which Germany had occupied in 1940. The Royal Navy had to provide this protection every time a convoy sailed for Russia.

The British destroyer HMS *Achates* was part of the protection for convoy JW 51 B. It was attacked on 31 December 1942 by a large German battle-cruiser – *Hipper*. A storm of well-aimed shells hit the British ship, badly damaging it and killing the Captain and 40 of the crew. The second-in-command, Lieutenant Peyton-Jones, immediately took control and ordered the engine room to create lots of smoke from its funnel and make a screen that the convoy and *Achates* could hide behind.

The smokescreen worked and *Hipper* sailed off to look for other targets. However, on board the crippled *Achates* the situation was very serious. The damage caused her to lean over and take on water, so much, that she capsized (rolled over) into the freezing ocean and quickly sank.

A person could survive for 30 seconds in the sea before freezing to death. Just before the ship went down, Peyton-Jones had been able to contact a nearby trawler, HM *Northern Gem*. Miraculously, 81 men out of a crew of 194 were rescued. Admiral Tovey said Peyton-Jones' actions had been 'gallant in the extreme'. Despite the terrible sacrifices made by the crew of the *Achates*, convoy JW 51 B successfully sailed into Murmansk, with all its precious war equipment intact, on 4 January 1943.

◄ **A Convoy entering Murmansk. The port was only 112 kilometres from the nearest Luftwaffe base.**

A SECOND THOUGHT

What would you dislike most about 'the worst journey in the world'?

A Freezing Journey

Winston Churchill called the voyage to Russia 'the worst journey in the world'. In winter, when there was only a couple of hours of daylight, the sea spray froze to the guns and rigging and the men had to chip it off immediately or the ship would capsize. If this wasn't bad enough, there were icebergs, sleet and snow to cope with, in temperatures of around -12 to -16°C. In spite of this, the ships carried millions of tons of essential war supplies to keep the war against Nazi Germany going.

▲ **Winston Churchill understood the importance of keeping the Soviet Union in the war.**

SPECIAL OPERATIONS

The Special Operations Executive - SOE - recruited men and women to work as agents in German-occupied Europe. They had to be brave, clever, independent and strong. Agents were trained and then parachuted into areas behind enemy lines to spy...

Name:
Krystina Gizycka/Christine Granville ('Pauline')

Date: 1939–44

Event: The 'Secret War'

Age: 31

Location: Europe

Medals: George Medal and OBE

Date Awarded:
2 September 1945 (GM);
May 1947 (OBE)

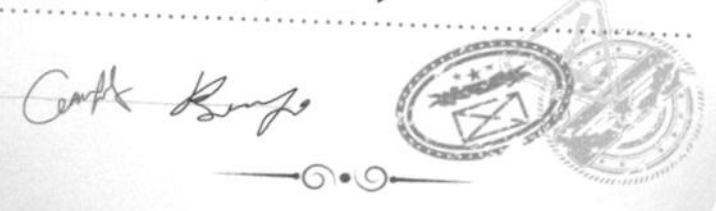

▲ Krystina's SOE photograph.

Krystina Gizycka was a Polish refugee. She was recruited and trained for work in occupied Europe. To do this she changed her name to Christine Granville and adopted the code name 'Pauline'. The SOE taught her to use a wireless/transmitter set, make a parachute jump, and use explosives, codes and personal disguises.

In 1940 'Pauline' was sent into Poland. Her mission was to act against German anti-British propaganda and to collect and transmit any intelligence she could learn. 'Pauline' also carried weapons, explosives, secret mail and large amounts of money. The risks were huge. If she was arrested with such equipment she could be tortured and shot as a spy.

Resistance

The Special Operations Executive was set up in July 1940 by Winston Churchill. The idea was to send in specially trained agents to encourage resistance in Nazi-occupied areas. Local resistance groups were extremely useful to the allied cause. For example, just after D-Day, French groups bombed roads, bridges and railways and cut telegraph wires in order to slow down the German reaction to the invasion in Normandy.

'Pauline' was based in Hungary, a dangerous place where the police were controlled by the Gestapo. She had to cross into Poland and Slovakia many times, which meant crossing the hazardous Tatra Mountains. In the bitter winter of 1940–41 she walked for six days through a blizzard in temperatures as low as -30°C!

'Pauline's' best piece of intelligence gathering was finding out that Germany planned to invade Russia in the summer of 1941. Although she was briefly arrested by the Gestapo, and brutally questioned, she managed to buy herself out.

Her finest moment came when she worked with the French Resistance in 1944. Three British agents were arrested by the Gestapo and were to be shot on the night of 17 August. 'Pauline' walked straight in and met with the Gestapo chief. She bluffed him with stories and eventually, the prisoners were released!

A LOINTAINES
B SONT
C MES
D AMOURS
E MERIDIONALES
F PERDUS
G MES
H SOUVENIRS
I DES
J HEUREUSES
K ANNEES
L L'OPPRESSION
M LA
N HAINE
O PASSIONS
P INFERNALES
Q MONT
R RAVI
S LE
T BONHEUR
U ET LA
V TRANQUILLITE
W JE
X VOUDRAIS
Y MAINTENANT
Z OUBLIER

II
A-QUITTANT
B-LES
C-FUMEES
D-LES
E-GRISAILLES
F-DES
G-VILLES
H-FUYANT
I-RAPIDEMENT
J-VERS
K-LES
L-GRANDES
M-ECHAPPEES
N-J'AI
O-TROUVE
P-LE
Q-BONHEUR
R-D'UNE
S-EXISTENCE
T-TRANQUILLE
U-AU
V-FOYER
X-D'UNE
Y-FEMME
Z-ADOREE
W-LUMINEUX

III
A-L'OCEAN
B-QUI
C-RESPIRE
D-LA
E-FEMME
F-QUI
G-SOUPIRE
H-L'ENFANT
J-VA
K-RIRE
L-REJOUISSENT
M-MON
N-COEUR
O-PLENITUDE
P-IMMENSE
Q-LA
S-QUI
T-COMMENCE
U-SECOULE
V-EN
W-SILENCE
X-PERFECTION
Y-DU
Z-BONHEUR

Krystina's code card.

A SECOND THOUGHT

SOE agents had very little chance of survival. Why did people still volunteer?

COMMANDO RAID

One of the most daring raids of the war took place on 28 March 1942 at the French port of St. Nazaire. An old destroyer, HMS *Campbeltown*, packed with explosives and escorted by smaller gunboats sailed from England heading for the dock gates.

Names: George Wheeler and Richard Sims
Date: March–May 1942
Event: Raid on St. Nazaire
Location: France
Medal: Military Medal
Date Awarded: 29 September 1942

The 622 men on board the flotilla were commandos determined to make the huge dock unusable for the dangerous German battleship *Tirpitz*. As HMS *Campbeltown* rammed the dock gates at 1.34 am, two commandos, Corporal George Wheeler and Lance Corporal Richard Sims, leapt from their gunboat onto the harbour wall. The Germans responded and the commandos took casualties. In the fierce fighting, Wheeler and Sims could not reach their target. They were told that evacuation was impossible and were ordered to fight their way through the town and into open country.

At 4 am they found their way into the town and hid in a dried-up drain. They waited for 18 hours while things died down, eating their chocolate rations. At 11 am that morning they heard a massive explosion. HMS *Campbeltown's* deadly cargo, with a delayed fuse, had blown up, completely wrecking the dock! They moved out at midnight and made for open country. Totally lost, without maps or food they hid in a

◀ The huge dock at St. Nazaire.

▲ **Some of the British commandos and sailors captured during the raid.**

haystack. A farmer discovered them in the morning and took them to his farmhouse, gave them food, civilian clothes and 250 francs!

They left at 11.30 pm, but soon became lost again. They slept in another haystack and were again discovered by a farmer who warned them of German patrols.

He provided them with breakfast and more importantly a map. They decided to head for the French border, get into Spain and make for the British base in Gibraltar.

With the help of civilians, skill, bravery and good fortune, the pair reached Toulouse in southwest France on 17 April. They contacted the local resistance who helped them into Spain and Gibraltar. They covered nearly 1,800 kilometres arriving back in Britain on 16 May 1942!

A SECOND THOUGHT

Faced with such a journey, would you travel at night or during the day? Why?

Battle of the Atlantic

This was one of the most important campaigns for Britain's survival in the war. Vast quantities of essential equipment, food and raw materials were sent to Britain by the USA, by Atlantic convoys. German submarines attacked them mercilessly, but Britain was also afraid that huge battleships, like the *Tirpitz*, would threaten this Atlantic 'lifeline'. The only dock big enough to give the *Tirpitz* a safe haven was at St. Nazaire and the success of the raid meant it was never used in the Atlantic.

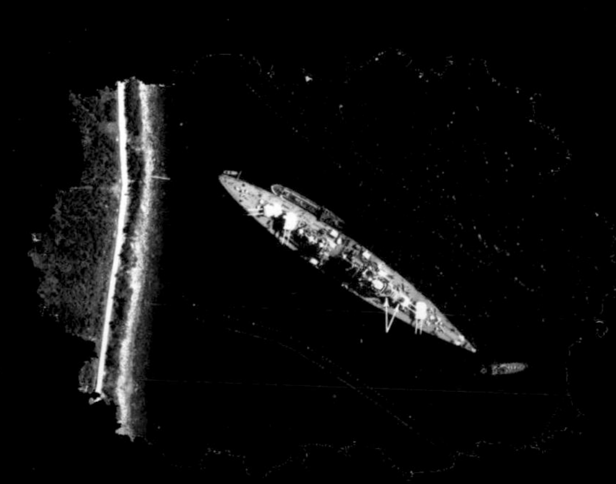

▲ ***Tirpitz*, one of Nazi Germany's most powerful battleships.**

THE GREAT ESCAPE

Name: Roger Bushell
Date: 24–26 March 1944
Event: The Great Escape
Location: Germany
Award: Mentioned in Despatches
Date Awarded: 13 June 1946

Dotted all over German-occupied Europe were the 'Stalags' or prisoner of war (POW) camps. Stalag Luft III was a camp run by the Luftwaffe and most of the prisoners were airmen. One of the captives was desperate to escape.

Roger Bushell was a brilliant athlete, fluent in French and German, and trained as a barrister. He was a member of the Auxiliary Air Force (Reserve) and when war broke out, he was put in charge of 92 Squadron flying Spitfires.

On 23 May 1940, as the Allies retreated to the coast, Bushell was flying in support and was shot down near Calais. He was captured and sent to Dulag Luft as a POW. He escaped in June 1941 but was re-captured just metres from the Swiss border. He escaped again and was recaptured in Prague and brutally questioned by the Gestapo. In October 1942, he was sent to Stalag Luft III.

Bushell devised an escape plan for up to 200 prisoners. Three tunnels were to be dug nine metres deep and code named 'Tom', 'Dick' and 'Harry'. If one was discovered, there would still be two to work on. Plans of the surrounding area were drawn, documents forged and civilian clothing made. 'Tom' was discovered in the summer of 1943, so all efforts were put into making 'Harry' operational.

On 24–25 March 1944, the Great Escape took place. Bushell paired up with French pilot Bernard Scheidhauer and, after leaving the tunnel exit, took cover in the woods. They made for Sagan railway station and caught the 3.30 am train to Breslau. Arriving at Saarbrucken on 26 March, they were promptly arrested.

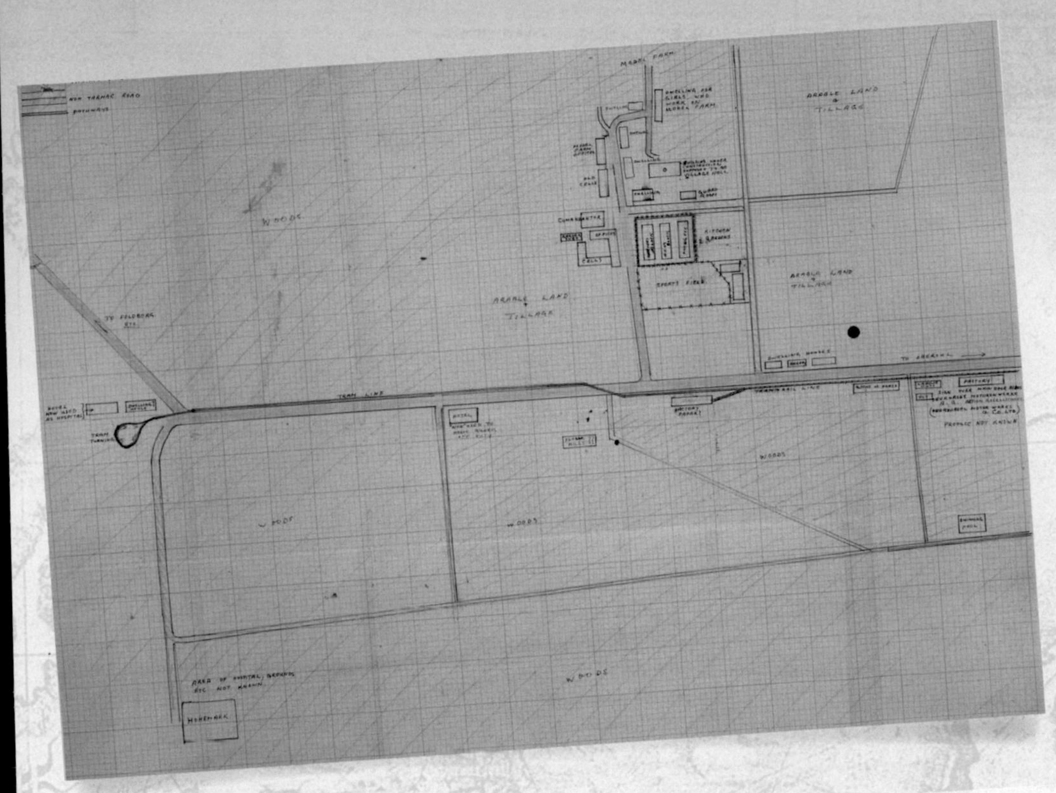

◀ It was important to make accurate sketches of the camp so the tunnels would be long enough.

Only 76 men actually escaped in the break-out and 73 were recaptured. On orders from Adolf Hitler, 50 of them were murdered by the Gestapo, including Roger Bushell and Bernard Scheidhauer.

A SECOND THOUGHT

The Gestapo told Bushell he would be executed if he continued escaping, so why do you think he still organised the Great Escape?

Planning to Escape

Roger Bushell believed it was a duty for POWs to try to escape captivity. He said many times that when a prisoner escaped, the Germans had to waste time and resources trying to catch them. If they were tracking escapees across Europe, they could not man the Atlantic Wall which was designed to stop an Allied invasion of the European coast. Bushell believed that escaping was a small but important contribution to the war effort.

▲ An aerial image of Stalag Luft III.

BEHIND ENEMY LINES

In 1942, the Japanese inflicted a serious defeat on British forces in Burma. Lieutenant Colonel Orde Wingate proposed that guerrilla forces could operate deep in the rainforest and attack the Japanese behind their lines.

Name: Jemadar Man Bahadur Gurung

Date: February–May 1943

Event: 1st Chindit Campaign

Location: Kyaithin, Burma

Medals: Indian Order of Merit

Date Awarded: 16 December 1943

On 8 February 1943, a 3,000-strong group called Chindits advanced into Burma. They were well equipped with air support, but would be fighting a long way from their base. Wingate called this tactic 'Long Range Penetration'. Part of the force was the 3/2nd Gurkha Rifles and one of its officers was Jemadar Man Bahadur Gurung from Nepal. ('Jemadar' is the equivalent of a Lieutenant).

Working their way carefully through the rainforest, the Chindits did not see any enemy troops, but when they started blowing up important railway track and bridges the Japanese began to hunt them down.

On the night of the 2/3rd March at Kyaikthin, Jemadar Gurung's column was ambushed by Japanese troops. At first there was chaos, as the Chindits did not know where the enemy was. With great coolness, while most of his column got away, Gurung made a stand and continued to engage the enemy. The return fire was aimed at him so the Japanese did not rush off and search for the other men. Using trees and the undergrowth as cover he managed to pin the enemy down. After a while, when things quietened down, he melted into the rainforest to re-join his group.

The next day, they headed eastwards in the hope of meeting other groups, carefully watching out for more ambushes or enemy activity. As well as his own, Jemadar Gurung collected several abandoned automatic weapons on the way. Not finding other Chindit columns, he led his party back to the safety of the Chindwin River.

Of the 3,000 troops who left in February, only 2,182 returned four months later. They had walked between 1,600 and 2,400 kilometres inside enemy territory. Not surprisingly, many men were in very poor condition.

▲ This painting shows the difficult conditions in the Burmese rainforest.

A SECOND THOUGHT

Try to imagine why fighting in the rainforest was so difficult and confusing.

▲ Specialist kit for Chindits fighting hundreds of miles behind enemy lines.

The Chindits

The Chindits were like guerrilla fighters, effective with 'hit and run' tactics. They attacked, caused damage and quickly disappeared back into the rainforest. The attack on the Mandalay-Myitkyina railway put it out of order for four weeks. The expedition proved that groups could operate in difficult terrain, deep behind enemy lines. A second Chindit expedition took place in 1944. It was specially trained in skills like river crossing, receiving air supply drops and attacking enemy villages. Each column contained a commando platoon specialising in demolitions and setting booby traps.

D-DAY

By 1944, the western Allies, Great Britain and the USA, were ready to invade German-occupied France. On 6 June, a huge armada of ships, landing craft and floating harbours crossed the English Channel.

Name: H.G. McKinlay
Date: 6 June 1944
Event: D-Day
Location: Normandy, France
Medal: Conspicuous Gallantry Medal
Date Awarded: 29 August 1944

The first troops landed on the Normandy beaches at 6.30 am in chaotic scenes. German forces, protected by their Atlantic Wall, tried to push the Allied soldiers back into the sea. Since 1940, they had built up strong coastal defences intended to make any invasion very difficult.

All morning the beaches were a frenzy of bullets and explosions. Petty Officer Henry McKinlay, a Royal Navy commando, was put ashore just after noon in the midst of the chaos. Diving for cover and looking at his map, he realised he had been dropped off in the wrong place.

▲ Anti-tank obstacles on the mined Normandy beaches.

McKinlay reckoned he was almost a kilometre from where he was supposed to rendezvous with his comrades. He carefully made his way along the beach, ducking and diving for cover from the deadly fire, when he came across a group of soldiers and sailors looking for the same place has him.

McKinlay took charge and explained what they would have to do. Suddenly, they were fired on by two machine-gun posts higher up the beach. Everyone

▲ **Commandos directing operations on the beaches.**

dived for cover while McKinlay snaked his way up the beach, closer to the enemy strong points. With the help of a couple of carefully lobbed hand grenades, these guns were silenced.

The group then carried on along the beach but bullets rang out again, hitting one of the soldiers. Snipers were trying to pick them off. McKinlay, under fire himself, was able to rescue the wounded man, get him to safety and tend to his wound.

A SECOND THOUGHT

Why might you feel nervous about landing on a flat and wide sandy beach?

The End of the War

McKinlay's job was to organise the landings so that the Allies could bring more men and equipment into the battle safely. In time the Allies spread out through France and in August, Paris was liberated. The success of D-Day meant that Nazi Germany could not win World War II. They were now trapped between the Soviet Red Army in the east and the Allies in the west. Caught in this vice, the German Army retreated and surrendered nearly a year later in May 1945.

▲ **A propaganda poster showing the powerful progress of the Allies.**

RESEARCH & RECORDS

The extraordinary people you have met in this book have all been decorated in some way for their acts of bravery and valour. However, how do we know these stories are true and what are they based on? How do we know 'Christine Granville' walked over the Tatra Mountains in -30°C? Where is the evidence that Daphne Pearson dragged a severely wounded pilot from a burning plane?

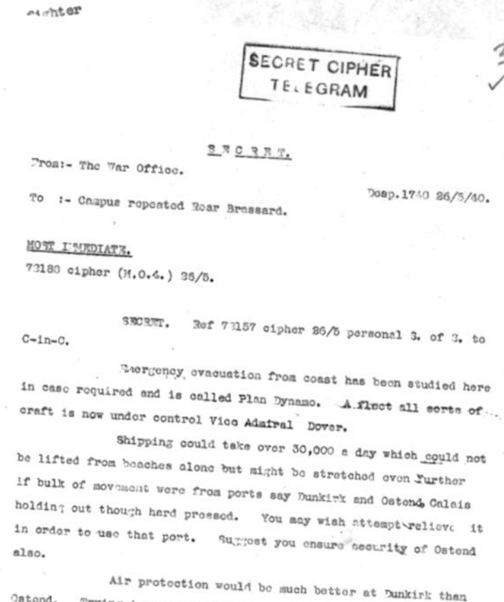

S E C R E T.

C I P H E R.

TO: MADELON
FROM: TROOPERS
No. 72794 of 1/6.
MOST IMMEDIATE

Following from Prime Minister to General SPEARS for General WEYGAND 72794 1st June.

Crisis in evacuation now reached.

Time of origin. 1853.
Time of receipt. 2010.
Completed. 2100.

SECRET CIPHER TELEGRAM

S E C R E T.

From:- The War Office.

To :- Caspus repeated Roar Brassard.

Desp.1740 26/5/40.

MOST IMMEDIATE.

73180 cipher (M.O.4.) 26/5.

SECRET. Ref 73157 cipher 26/5 personal 3. of 3. to C-in-C.

Emergency evacuation from coast has been studied here in case required and is called Plan Dynamo. A fleet all sorts of craft is now under control Vice Admiral Dover.

Shipping could take over 30,000 a day which could not be lifted from beaches alone but might be stretched even further if bulk of movement were from ports say Dunkirk and Ostend, Calais holding out though hard pressed. You may wish attempt relieve it in order to use that port. Suggest you ensure security of Ostend also.

Air protection would be much better at Dunkirk than Ostend. Trying improve communications Dunkirk - Dover.

It is not repeat not intended to send Canadians Dunkerque Bastion has no cipher. Please repeat to them.

C.4. (Telegrams)

Copies to:- S. of S.
C.I.G.S.
Q.M.G.
V.C.I.G.S.
M.O.4.7.
Q(M)2.
Capt.Jeffery, 15 North Block,1, Admiralty. (2 copies).
D.M.C. Air Ministry.

To learn about the past historians must look for evidence. For example, if they wanted to research the evacuation at Dunkirk in 1940, they would study official government and military documents, film and photographic evidence and personal writings like diaries and letters of the time. They might even try and speak to a soldier who was there at the time.

◀ **Documents like these provide important information about the events at Dunkirk in 1940.**

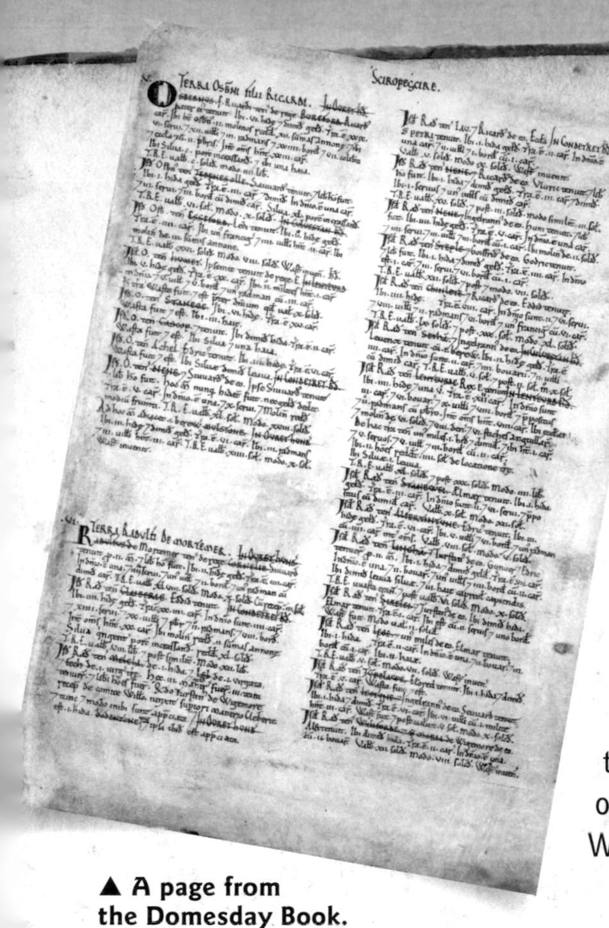

▲ A page from the Domesday Book.

Important documents are kept safe at an archive. There are archives in every country all over the world. One of the biggest is The National Archives in Kew, London. Historical documents from the government are stored here, as well as other material such as photographs, posters, maps, drawings and paintings. They even have electronic and digital files. The range of material stretches back over 1000 years, and they even have the Domesday Book! This is a survey of England completed in 1086 by William the Conqueror.

▲ Researchers at The National Archives take care when handing very old documents!

Holding a piece of actual historical evidence is very exciting. It can tell you things you expect, but it can also tell you unusual things. For example, a government file might tell you what was decided about the numbers of planes in the Battle of Britain, but it might also hint at the arguments between ministers and departments in coming to the decision. Historians call this 'witting' and 'unwitting' testimony.

GLOSSARY

ally – A country with an agreement to defend another.

altitude – Height above sea level or, in a plane, the land.

armada – A large number of ships together at sea.

Bf 109 – A German fighter plane used in World War II.

Bf 110 – A German heavy fighter used in World War II.

blitzkrieg – A German word meaning 'lightning war'.

commando – A member of a military group that carries out swift attacks in enemy territory.

conscription – When a person is called up to do compulsory military service.

convoy – A group of vessels sailing together at the speed of the slowest ship.

evacuation – To take people away from a dangerous place.

flotilla – A group of boats or small ships.

franc – The French currency before the euro.

gallantry – Strong courage in the face of danger or difficulty.

Gestapo – Nazi Germany's secret police.

guerrilla – Fighters who makes sudden attacks on a bigger force or army. From the Spanish, meaning 'little war'.

intelligence – In military terms, information about your enemy.

Ju 87 – Known as the 'Stuka', this was a German dive bomber used in World War II.

Lancaster – The RAF's main heavy bomber in World War II.

Luftwaffe – The air force of Nazi Germany.

propaganda – Information that is one-sided in an effort to influence people.

resistance – People who fight back against an occupying army.

selfless – A person who thinks about the well-being others before him/herself.

sniper – Someone who shoots at people from a hidden position.

strategic bombing – Bombing that tries to harm a nation's ability to fight a war.

vice – A tool that has two jaws for holding.

FURTHER INFORMATION

BOOKS

World War II Sourcebook: Soldiers
by Charlie Samuels, Wayland (2011)

Machines and Weaponry of World War II
by Charlie Samuels, Wayland (2013)

In the War: The Blitz
by Simon Adams, Wayland (2010)

Battle of Britain – A Second World War Spitfire Pilot 1939–1941 (My Story),
by Chris Priestley, Scholastic (2008)

WEBSITES

www.nationalarchives.gov.uk
Website of The National Archives.

www.nationalarchives.gov.uk/education/world-war-two.htm
The National Archives' educational page for World War II.

www.bbc.co.uk/schools/primaryhistory/world_war2/
BBC Learning site about World War II.

www.spartacus.schoolnet.co.uk/2WW.htm
Lots of information about World War II with a section on individual soldiers.

INDEX

9780750279703

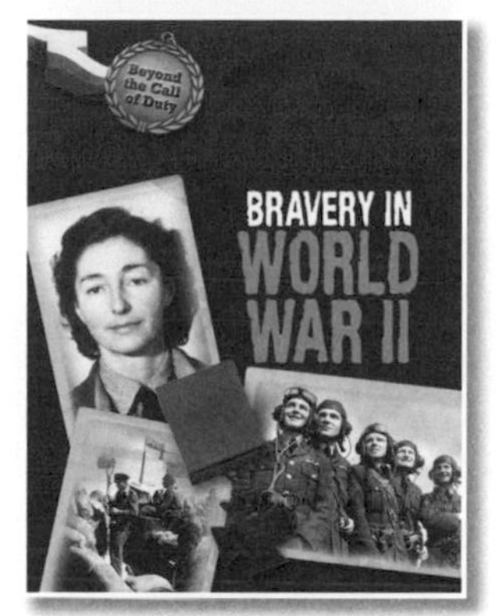

9780750279734

9780750279710

9780750279727

CONTENTS OF TITLES IN THE SERIES

BRAVERY IN WORLD WAR I

What is Bravery?
Opening Moves
Trench Raid
A Long Way From Home
Front-line Nurses
The War in the Air
The War at Sea
Trench Warfare
War Workers
Walter Tull – Unrecognised Hero
Tank Against Tank
Stretcher Bearer
Research and Records

BRAVERY IN WORLD WAR II

What is Bravery?
Dunkirk Evacuation
The Battle of Britain
Blitz!
Dam Busters
Women's War Work
Atlantic Convoys
Special Operations
Commando Raid
The Great Escape
Behind Enemy Lines
D-Day
Research and Records

CIVILIAN BRAVERY IN THE WORLD WARS

What is Bravery?
Trapped Behind Enemy Lines
The Lady on the Black Horse
Death from the Sky
An Awful Splendour
Legion d'Honneur
Blitz
Firefighter
Shark-infested Waters
Hull Had No Peace
Ammunition Train
Beyond Human Endurance
Research and Records

ANIMAL BRAVERY IN WARTIME

What is Bravery?
Dog Training School
Patrols and Parachutes
Horses at the Front
A Lucky Charm
Small Bird, Big Heart
Special Agent Pigeon
The Other War Horses
Gallantry on all Fronts
The Heavy Brigade
The Soldier Bear
One of the Family
Research and Records